William Macdonald Sinclair

Chapters in the Christian life

William Macdonald Sinclair

Chapters in the Christian life

ISBN/EAN: 9783741136832

Manufactured in Europe, USA, Canada, Australia, Japa

Cover: Foto ©Andreas Hilbeck / pixelio.de

Manufactured and distributed by brebook publishing software (www.brebook.com)

William Macdonald Sinclair

Chapters in the Christian life

CHAPTERS IN THE CHRISTIAN LIFE.

By W. M. Sinclair, D.D.,
Archdeacon of London.

LONDON: JAMES CLARKE & CO.,
13 & 14, Fleet Street. 1897.

First Edition, November, 1897.
Reprinted from THE CHRISTIAN WORLD.

TO THE VENERATED MEMORY
OF
JOHN SINCLAIR,
THIRTY-THREE YEARS
ARCHDEACON OF MIDDLESEX
AND
VICAR OF KENSINGTON,
AND UPWARDS OF THIRTY YEARS
SECRETARY AND TREASURER
OF THE
NATIONAL SOCIETY FOR THE EDUCATION
OF THE POOR.
1797—1875.

Contents.

	PAGE
Is Life Worth Living?	1
The Illumination of Life	14
The Star of Christ	26
Indecision	45
Confession and Denial	54
A Good Conscience	63
Glimpses of Peace	80
The True Meat	98
The Next Generation	116

Chapters in the Christian Life.

Is Life Worth Living?

*Therefore now, O Lord, take away, I beseech Thee, my life; for it is better for me to die than to live. Then said the Lord, Doest thou well to be angry?—*JONAH IV. 3.

THE moody discontent of Jonah has been repeated in every age. Who does not know some gloomy Rebekah who, when Esau married against her wishes, exclaimed, "I am weary of my life! What good shall my life to do unto me?" "My soul chooseth death rather than life," was the perpetual complaint of Job. "Let the day perish wherein I was born!" "Oh, that I might have my request, and that God would grant me the thing

The Facts of Discontent.

which I long for! even that it would please God to destroy me; that He would let loose His hand and cast me off!" "It is enough," cried Elijah; "now take away my life; for I am not better than my fathers." "I hated life," says Solomon in the Book of Ecclesiastes. There has been plenty of this feeling in literature and history. "The happiest hour of life is the departure from it," said Calanus, the Hindu companion of Alexander the Great. "Life is a continuation of misery," said Acosta the Portuguese. "I doubt," wrote Seneca, "if any one would accept life if he knew what it would cost him." "The blessings of life," wrote Pliny the Elder, "are not equal to its ills, even though the number of the two were equal; nor can any pleasure compensate for the least pain." And in our own times men who have lost faith in the future are constantly asking the dismal question, "Is life worth living?" Poets have written in this strain:—

What is the existence of man's life
But open war or slumbrous strife?
Where sickness to his sense presents
The combat of the elements?
And never feels a perfect peace
Till death's cold hand signs his release?

. . . . .

It is a weary interlude
Which doth short joys, long woes
  include—
The world, the stage; the prologue,
  tears;
The acts, vain hopes and varied fears;
The scene shuts up with loss of breath,
And leaves no epilogue but death.

Now the reason of all this dis- *The*
content and despair, this wishing *Explana-*
that you had never been born, this *tion.*
idea that you would be glad if you
could lie down and die, is simply
this: The people who fancy that
they feel these things, and who utter
these loud lamentations, are just
those who have not made a proper
use of life, or who have not understood what life really means. They

have employed it badly, and are sensitive to the discomforts of what they have done. But even these very people, unless they are in the sudden madness and frenzy of suicide, would be terribly scared if you should take them at their word. If you should suddenly meet them with a cup of poison, and should tell them that there was nothing for it but that they should drink it off at that moment, they would wring their hands, and sweat with horror, and cry aloud that they never meant what they said. Depend upon it, many a man who has jumped into a river has wished that he was out again before he was drowned. The assumed desire for death is only a strong way of saying that they are unhappy. They are unhappy because they have ruined their health, or because they are burdened by the yoke of bad habits, or because they have not discovered or been willing to learn what is the only way of being really happy. Solomon, for example, had forgotten his own wisdom, and surfeited himself with luxurious self-indulgence. Unless some mistake has crept into the Hebrew manuscript, it appears that he exceeded even Eastern licence in the scale of his domestic relations. So vast a family was enough to make any man thoroughly weary of the ceaseless monotony of unchecked gratification.

God gave the answer to Jonah. "Then said the Lord, Doest thou well to be angry?" He showed him that he might consider himself more than happy in having been chosen to be the means of saving 120,000 persons in the mighty city of Nineveh. The repentance of the city, the renewed healthiness of a vigorous municipal life, the simple joys of each quiet hearth and home rescued, restored, and refined by the influence of the wild Hebrew

The Remedy Lies in Union with the Omnipotent.

prophet: these things were enough to fill him with delight if he realised them and reflected on them properly. The answer is true for all time. Why is it that there are people who bless God for every minute that they live? Whether they are rich or poor the mere fact of living gives them such delight that they can never be too grateful for it. What is the meaning of it? Why are they different from the discontented? It is not merely that they are naturally sanguine and cheerful. Ill-health may produce morbid conditions, but it cannot rival the Holy Spirit of God in influencing the whole tenor of a life. David knew the secret, and he has written it out for us over and over again in words that can never be rivalled: "Thou wilt make me to know the path of life; in Thy presence is fulness of joy; at Thy right hand there are pleasures for evermore." And another Psalmist: "O, bless our

God, ye people, and make the voice of His praise to be heard: Which holdeth our soul in life, and suffereth not our feet to be moved." "Bless the Lord, O my soul," said David again (and he had plenty of troubles), "and all that is within me bless His holy Name. Bless the Lord, O my soul, and forget not all His benefits: Who forgiveth all thine iniquities, and healeth all thy diseases; Who redeemeth thy life from destruction; Who crowneth thee with loving-kindness and tender mercies."

The secret, then, is to put our life into God's hands; to follow His way of arranging it instead of our own; to take His will instead of the perverse, wayward, mischievous will which we find in our own minds; to live for others instead of for ourselves. "The end of life," said Socrates, "is to be like unto God; and the soul, following God, will be like unto

Effects of this Union on Life.

Him; He being the beginning, the middle, and the end of all things." "This span of life was lent for lofty duties, not for selfishness; not to be whiled away for aimless dreams, but to improve ourselves and to serve mankind."* Even Epicurus, the Greek philosopher, who is so much misrepresented because he tried to teach men to live for true pleasure, said that "it is impossible to live pleasurably without living prudently, honourably, and justly; and it is equally impossible to live prudently, honourably, and justly without living pleasurably." "To complain that life has no joys while there is a single creature whom we can relieve by our bounty, assist by our counsels, or enliven by our presence, is to lament the loss of that which we possess, and is just as reasonable as to die of thirst with the cup in our hands." † That is absolute

*Aubrey de Vere. †W. Melmoth.

truth. That is the teaching of Christ. That is the secret of life.

> He lives, who lives to God alone,
> And all are dead beside;
> For other source than God is none
> Whence life can be supplied.
>
> To live to God is to requite
> His love as best we may,
> To make His precepts our delight,
> His promises our stay.
>
> But life within a narrow ring,
> Of giddy joys comprised,
> Is falsely named, and no such thing,
> But rather death disguised.

If, then, you wish to be truly grateful for the benefit of living, and to be able to say sincerely that you praise God for your creation, preservation, and all the blessings of this life, you have only to follow the secret of David: Live not for yourself, but for God; and that means living for others. There is no happiness so great as the feeling that each day you have been doing something kind and useful; no discontent so gnaw-

The Secret of Happiness.

ing as the knowledge that you have been wasting your time, energies, and money on empty fancies, which were mere delusions, and left you poorer in all these things than before. Selfishness is the one great curse of our natures. It is a curse, because it can never be satisfied; because it makes everybody whom we meet an opponent; and because the object which it worships—ourselves—is so worthless. "Remember for what purpose you were born, and through the whole of life look at its end; and consider, when that comes, in what will you put your trust. Not in the bubble of worldly vanity—it will be broken; not in worldly pleasures — they will be gone; not in great connections—they cannot serve you; not in wealth—you cannot carry it away with you; not in rank—in the grave there is no distinction; not in the recollection of a life spent in giddy conformity to the silly fashions of a thoughtless and wicked world; but in that of a life spent soberly, righteously, and godly, in the path of duty."

The Dignity and Glory of Life.

Life is infinitely more than a mere consciousness of existence, to be moulded by the customs of the day, and to be spent on the advancement and cultivation of self for the purposes of the visible being merely, even in any of the myriad aspects which self presents. "The mere lapse of years is not life. To eat and drink and sleep, to be exposed to darkness and to the light, to pace round in the mill of habit and turn thought into an implement of trade—this is not life! Knowledge, truth, love, beauty, goodness, faith, alone can give vitality to the mechanism of existence. The life of mirth which vibrates through the heart, the tears which freshen the dry wastes within, the music which brings childhood back, the prayer which calls the future near, the doubt which makes us meditate, the death which startles us with mystery, the hardship which forces us to struggle, the anxiety which ends in trust—these are the true nourishment of our mere natural being." To the mind which is set on the future in obedience to the will of God, and which is therefore living the life of duty and the life of love, all these things bring joy. They supply new experience, new self-control, new wisdom, new victories, new faith, new knowledge of God and of the truth. If ever we are tempted, like Jonah, to grumble and repine, to make light of the privilege of living, loving, and working for God, and to say, "Therefore now, O Lord, take, I beseech Thee, my life from me, for it is better for me to die than to live," then it is in such truths and thoughts as these that the Lord reminds us of what is really the fact of the case, and says to us, " Doest thou well to be angry? By calling on thee to work for Me and for thy fellows, have I not given thee a share in the life of Me, the omnipotent God, Who am Light, and Love, and Bliss, and Perfection, at Whose right hand there are pleasures for evermore?"

The Illumination of Life.

Love worketh no ill to his neighbour.
ROMANS xv. 30.

Intellectual and Practical Benevolence.

IT is a very easy thing for us to see from Holy Scripture that a universal kindness and benevolence is the true spirit of Christianity. We are quite ready to say that this was what made the life of ~~Christ~~ ~~Son of God~~ so supremely attractive, because He had this quality in a Divine degree. We know that each of the Epistles of St. Paul and his colleagues is full of the most urgent exhortations to the cultivation of this temper. The Epistles of St. John breathe it from beginning to end, and stir us to our inmost hearts when we read them. But, all the same, it is quite possible for us to know

THE ILLUMINATION OF LIFE. 15

these things well enough in our heads, and yet to be harsh, cold, selfish, and inconsistent in our own daily way of living. There is a wonderful amount of the true kindness of Jesus Christ about in our day, but there is not enough of it in each individual parish and congregation. If any one parish or congregation could give themselves up each without reserve to the guiding of God in their whole dealings with others, the effect would be to bring us very near to the gates of heaven.

The obstacle to the possibility of the loving spirit of the Lord Jesus taking complete possession of the heart of each of us is the selfishness which is born in all alike, and which is our strongest natural characteristic. It is perfectly true that the seeds of kind feeling are present in every heart waiting to be developed. Nobody can deny that there is not one single person born into the world

Natural Selfishness Stronger than Natural Benevolence.

who is utterly and entirely hard-hearted. But selfishness, or self-interest, or the desire to please ourselves is there also; and by the long habits of the human race, and by the force of example all round, and by the cleverness of the devil in tempting and deceiving us, it is a far stronger root than the seeds of kindness,if left to themselves. It grows more quickly, and if not checked it rapidly fills the heart, chokes every other growth, and excludes every happier impulse.

The Desire to Get On.
Everybody, for instance, by nature wants to get on. Life may, from the point of view of nature, be considered a struggle of those who are trying to elbow each other out in the pursuit of good things. Everybody wants to have good things for himself, or for those who are a part of himself. Nobody by nature would wish to remain in the background, and not to get any of the good things which

THE ILLUMINATION OF LIFE. 17

are to be had, if he can only have the pleasure of helping other people to get them instead.

The Desire for Amusement.

Everybody by nature wishes to be amused and satisfied. Everybody by nature wishes to indulge himself in what he has found will give him pleasure, or what he thinks will minister to his enjoyment. He wishes, for instance, to be enlivened by going constantly to the theatre, and he does not consider that those who are employed at the theatres are necessarily exposed to more severe trials of their virtue than others are. He wishes to dine well and to dress well every day, and he does not remember that there are multitudes round him who are in constant suffering and unceasing distress, and who need all that he can possibly spare for their relief. Or he wants to aggrandise his family, and he gives little or nothing to the poor. Or he indulges himself in vice, and never bestows a thought on the serious question whether, besides doing harm to himself, he is not hardening the hearts of the unfortunate sharers in his unlawful pleasures, and binding the chains of the devil still more firmly round their dark and unhappy souls. Or he wishes to be always very merry and amusing, and he never reflects whether his words and jokes and jests may not be helping, each time he opens his lips, to keep others away from the feet of the Lord Jesus Christ. In all these and countless other ways we see how far easier it is for men to be selfish, and to work ill to their neighbours, than to be loving and kind in the Christian sense of the words.

Natural Affection not necessarily Christian Virtue.

Nor must such persons deceive themselves by sometimes feeling touches of natural affection. Such touches are beautiful marks of the wisdom of the Creator in animal life, and have little or nothing to do in the contest of the soul between selfishness and benevolence. There is hardly an animal in which the instinct of the mother for her young is not for a time exceedingly strong. Some of the most beautiful pictures in natural history might be seen in the hen fighting for her chickens against tremendous odds, or the grouse on the moor pretending to be lame and risking her own life that she may conceal the place where her little ones are feeding, or the swallow searching all day for food for her young, or the cow filling the whole valley with her wild and plaintive moans in her agony when her calf has been taken from her. A man must be very far gone indeed in ~~wickedness and devilry~~ if he feels no pang at the loss of ~~a tender~~ one ~~mother, or a wife~~ whom he has ~~once~~ loved, or a brother or a ~~friend~~ with whom he has been long associated, and from whom he has received kind deeds and words. But these feelings, ~~and the feeling~~

~~which makes a man admire~~ and
~~court a woman,~~ are mere natural
impulses. They may be raised by
Christian thought and discipline
into the highest, purest, and most
lovely of virtues, but in themselves
they have little or nothing to do
with Christian virtue, or with the
struggle between right and wrong,
and must not be taken as in themselves signs of a regenerate nature.
A man may be just as selfish for
his mother or his wife or his children as he is on his own account.
His natural affection for them,
unless properly disciplined by the
law and spirit of the Lord Jesus
Christ, may make him quite as
unjust and hard to other people as
he would be made by his own
interest. It is not by pointing to
mere natural affection, or good
fellowship, or friendship, that a
man can excuse himself for his
general selfishness, or lay claim to
be on the right side in the struggle
between good and evil.

THE ILLUMINATION OF LIFE. 21

The fact is, that the real and true Christian charity, or love, or kindness, or benevolence is, like every other grace, the free gift of God, and can only be had by asking Him earnestly and directly and intentionally for it. Nothing but His Holy Spirit, seriously prayed for by ourselves, can subdue our natural selfishness. We may try as hard as we like to discipline ourselves, but if we have given up our prayers and never ask God for anything, then we shall go on just like the rest of the world, doing whatever pleases us most, whether on the spur of the moment or after careful calculation, and never caring to stop and consider how our conduct in things small and great affects the welfare of other people.

Christian Love the Gift of God.

But this gift has to be obtained, this lesson has to be learnt, if we are to be true Christians. Nothing can be clearer from the teaching of the New Testament. It is a hard thing to our perverted wills, and

The Gift can be Sought and Obtained.

will need long and frequent petitions to the Giver of all good gifts. It will need constant watching when we have once found that beautiful and healthy grace growing in our hearts and suggesting to us to think of others before ourselves. But it is the only and true sign of the Christian spirit and temper, and it must be ours if we are to enter the kingdom of heaven. Nothing is too hard for God. His power and grace can soften the most worldly heart when it is once turned to him. Him that cometh unto Him He will in no wise cast out. If ye, being evil, know how to give good gifts unto your children, how much more shall your heavenly Father give the Holy Spirit to them that ask Him?

This Spirit is the Touchstone of Genuine Christian Life.

By this spirit of love shall we know that we are Christ's disciples. Like Christ, we shall never fail to be touched by the feeling of the infirmities of those about us.

THE ILLUMINATION OF LIFE. 23

Like Him, we shall try each day to fill up our whole time by doing good. Like Him, we shall wish others to get riches and honours and happiness and comforts and all manner of things that are good rather than ourselves. Like Him, we shall not be troubling about high or great people, but bending down to take our share of the troubles of the lowliest. Like Him, we shall think nothing of worldly advancement or consideration or honour, but look only for the honour which comes from Him in the answer of a conscience which is at once awake and at rest. We shall be forbearing and patient, and eager only to make everybody happy. We shall be free from the torments of envy and jealousy. We shall never boast or speak of ourselves, or refer to our own doings and glory. We shall never bring dishonour on the name of our Lord by inconsistent or unpleasant or ugly behaviour. We shall never have objects of our own which would clash with the welfare of other people. We shall not easily be put out. We shall check ourselves in that dark, suspicious temper which is always on the look-out for slights and wrongs and ill-doings in others. Our pleasure will not be in proving others to be less good than they appear, or in gloating over tales of crime, sin, and imperfection. We shall be ready to endure unkindness and opposition and misunderstanding without discouragement. We shall believe the best of people till the contrary is proved. We shall hope ever more earnestly for the dawn of the perfect day which is coming. While we are still on earth we shall not be always looking for luxury and comfort, but we shall prefer to endure hardness as good soldiers of Jesus Christ.

Priceless Results. So our way will ever be growing brighter and happier, because ever more completely after the will of God and in harmony with His Divine energy. So all that is base in us will be more and more thoroughly subdued; and at last we shall pass into the land of perfect light and perfect love, where all will be delight and unutterable content, because there will be no unregenerate will, and no coldness or deadness or selfishness of heart to trouble us any more, for ever!

The Star of Christ.

> Then came wise men from the East, saying, Where is He that is born King of the Jews? for we have seen His star in the East, and are come to worship Him.—ST. MATT. II. 1, 2.

Composition of the Gospels.

THE relation by St. Matthew of the visit of the wise men from the East illustrates for us in a noticeable manner the principles in accordance with which we believe the Apostles and Evangelists to have been directed in the compilation of their narratives by the Holy Spirit of God. They were not compelled to write every event or saying in the same order, the same words, or with the same object. Amongst the innumerable incidents which might have been chronicled, each was permitted to record anything which he remembered most vividly, which had struck his own mind most forcibly, or which suited best his purpose and point of view. St. Mark, whose Gospel is for some unknown local reason brief and compressed, introduces our Lord in full manhood at the opening of His mission. St. Luke, who seems to have known that the events given by St. Matthew were already current among the churches, proposed from the most careful investigations to add what was not yet written down. Their independence and their variety are seen in the materials which they choose from the myriad circumstances of the birth and childhood of our Lord. St. Matthew, laying his chief stress on the kingly office of Jesus of Nazareth as the Messiah and the Son of David, seizes in the most natural way on the first recognition of that character by the wise men from the East. St. Luke, describing the Son of Man in His sympathy with common men, in His compassion on the poor and humble, prefers as naturally that his Gospel should not be without the familiar and oft-repeated episode of the manifestation to the shepherds on the hills of Bethlehem.

Simplicity of the Narrative.

The simplicity and directness of the language, the absence of all attempt at explanation or exaggeration, the almost bare relation of the mere facts themselves, with no other feeling than the unconscious conviction of their entire fitness, are in remarkable contrast to the wild tales and legends which in a later age gathered round the original lives of Christ, and which formed that strange and weird witness to the candour and sincerity of the New Testament which is known as the Apocryphal Gospels.

Walking by Faith, not by Sight.

In all consideration of the earthly life of our Lord and of the documents and authorities on which our acquaintance with it rests, we must remember that in every point of our religion it is emphatically true that we walk by faith and not by sight. The Gospels are better authenticated than any other book that ever was written; but if our grounds for accepting their Divine origin and truthfulness amounted actually to absolute demonstration, there would be no more room for belief. God has given us evidences of their inspiration and of their genuineness which are the strongest possible confirmations of our faith; but to attempt to place religion upon a scientific basis shows an ignorance of its essential nature. All that our experience of God's manner of revealing Himself to us teaches us to look for is that nothing should be presented to us which could be shown to be contradictory to fact. Accepting St. Matthew's Gospel as the inspired word of God for abundant and satisfactory reasons, we receive on his testimony alone the record of the visit of the wise men from the East.

Suetonius, Tacitus, Josephus.

But that such a visit was in itself highly probable can be shown from other sources. That a general expectation of some great deliverer to arise in the land of the Hebrews was current at this time is a matter recorded in secular literature. The Roman historian, Suetonius, writing about seventy years after the birth of Christ, said that "a firm persuasion had long prevailed throughout all the East that it was fated for the empire of the world to fall into the hands of one who should go forth from Judæa." Tacitus, a contemporary of Suetonius, speaks to the same effect. "Most of the Jews," he says, "were deeply impressed with the belief that the ancient writings of the priests would come to pass, and that at that very time should go forth from Judæa they who should be the rulers of the world." Suetonius and Tacitus, indeed, applied this to the Emperor Vespasian; but it is the long-sealed expectation which they record that is of value to us, not the particular and temporary reference which they themselves gave it. And the Hebrew historian Josephus, who lived a little before Suetonius and Tacitus, and who wrote about the wars of the Jews with the Romans which ended in the destruction of Jerusalem, tells us how what most cheered on his countrymen in undertaking that disastrous struggle was a mysterious oracle that was found in their sacred writings, how about that time one from their own country should become governor of the whole habitable earth.

To the East itself, whether that wide expression here means Persia or Chaldæa, it is more than possible that some form of the ancient *Balaam, Zoroaster.*

prophecy of Balaam may have survived, how that there should come a star out of Jacob, and a sceptre should rise out of Israel. The writings of Daniel at the Court of Babylon would be known to the learned in those countries. And the traditional predictions ascribed to their own prophet Zoroaster led them to expect a succession of three deliverers, two working as prophets to reform the world and raise up a kingdom, the third, Zoziosh, the greatest of the three, coming to be the head of the kingdom, to conquer the power of Darkness, and to raise the dead. These redeemers in strange fantastic ways they had connected with the seed of Abraham; and as their minds were thus in an attitude of attention, their contact with a people cherishing like hopes on stronger grounds may have prepared them to see in a king of the Jews the saviour for whom they looked.

THE STAR OF CHRIST.

The Heavens from the Plains of Chaldæa.

The great plains of Chaldæa and Persia, with their vast horizons and their deep, clear, tranquil nights, have always been the home of patient observation of the stars. Countless in number, fathomless in mystery, rolling round in their stately cadence, advancing and receding, crossing and declining, as in the silent rhythm of a majestic measure, they seemed to speak of the power of God and the destinies of men. From the beginning of the creation their voiceless sound had been going forth into all the earth, their unspoken words to the ends of the world; from the beginning of the creation day had been uttering speech unto day, and night unto night had been showing knowledge. There was neither speech nor language when their voice was not heard. The wise men in Egypt, in China, in Chaldæa and in Persia were profoundly impressed with their mystery and their importance, and

thus laid the foundations of
astronomical science. It is true
that they connected their observations with prognostications of the
future and occult influences over
human life. It is true that
astrology became a deceptive and
mischievous pursuit. But just as
chemistry sprang from alchemy,
just as even war gave rise to the
law of nations, so ancient pagan
astrology was the parent of our
modern science of astronomy.
And the tendency of all true
science is to point the way to
faith. A perception of the harmonious order of the firmament,
and especially a knowledge of the
movements of the heavenly bodies,
would direct devout minds to Him
who is the centre and sun of the
spiritual system, to the Creative
Word, the Source of all order.
Their study of the stars was used
as the instrument of advancing
and directing their faith. God
has always employed human means

THE STAR OF CHRIST.

in advancing His work amongst mankind, and He has never guaranteed that such human means should be from error. All secular knowledge, however mixed with mistakes, serves to draw minds turned towards the light to the Fountain of all Light. Error is but the husk, truth is the kernel. The star which, whatever it was, was a sign to these devout and learned watchers, is to us a symbol that all nature, the starry heavens and the whole compass of natural science, if reverently and patiently studied and properly understood, without hasty hypothesis, will, under the enlightenment of the Holy Spirit of God, lead to deeper and stronger faith.

What the star was, the serene simplicity of the unquestioning record of St. Matthew does not even suggest. The great astronomer Kepler in the seventeenth century discovered that there was, somewhere about the date of the *Recorded Sidereal Phenomena.*

birth of our Lord, a remarkable conjunction of the planets Jupiter and Saturn, which occurred three times at short intervals in one year, and he conjectured that, as in the case of such a threefold conjunction which occurred again in the year 1603, an intermittant star may have flared between them. It is stated that in the astronomical tables of the Chinese a record has been preserved that a new star did appear at that very period. But it is simpler for us who believe the Gospel histories to suppose that the light which roused such intense and unparalleled interest in the minds of these sages as they scanned the heavens from their watchtowers in the far East was truly other than natural; and that He who, at so momentous an event in the history of mankind, made glory shine over the hills of Bethlehem at midnight such that the host of heaven were seen praising God, made also a ray of the same heavenly splendour to gleam on those who in their own way were also seeking His truth.

What was the result of the mission of the company of wise men when they returned to their homes in the East we do not know. Churches were founded in Apostolic times amongst the Parthians, Medes, Persians and Chaldæans. In the fourth century we find the Emperor Constantine writing to the famous King Sapor the Second on behalf of his Christian subjects. But when war broke out with his son Constantine, the Magi of that day easily roused the king's suspicion against those who held the religion of the Roman Empire, and Symeon, the Bishop of the Persians, suffered martyrdom in a forty years' persecution. In the next century it was in Persia that the Nestorians found refuge, and

Beginnings of Persian and Chaldæan Christianity.

founded a Christendom of their own with a patriarch and twenty-five Metropolitans in different countries under his direction. The Nestorian Church did its best to redeem the suspicion of heresy which hung about it by the missionary zeal which spread Christianity from Persia to Arabia and India, Tartary and China. With their religion they diffused Greek and other learning, and founded schools and hospitals. It was from a Nestorian monk, Sergius by name, that Mohammed is supposed to have derived his knowledge of Christianity; the sect, protected by him, imparted to the Arabians much of the culture which they in their turn have brought back to the West, and which we now enjoy. In India the Nestorian missionaries from Persia have left the permanent fruit of their labours in the Christians of the Malabar coast, who reverence the memory of Theodore and Nestorius in their Syriac liturgy, and own subjection to the Nestorian patriarchs. They form a community of about 70,000 souls. Very slight traces of Nestorian Christianity are left in Tartary and China. In their chief seats on the Tigris and Euphrates the Nestorians were cruelly persecuted by the Mongols, and were almost exterminated by Tamerlane at the end of the fourteenth century. A remnant still remain in Kurdistan and Armenia, under a patriarch who has his seat in a retired valley on the borders of Turkey and Persia. They are a poor and ignorant people, and have been much reduced by war, plague, and cholera. They are willing recipients of the teaching of men of God from England and America; and hopes are entertained that they may be the best means for again spreading the faith of the Kingdom of Christ amongst their neighbours, as their ancestors did amongst the heathen of the ancient world.

The Gifts of Christ in Christian Civilisation.

I have thought that these details would interest you in connection with the impressive memories of the second chapter of St. Matthew's Gospel. But it is still more important for us to carry the parallel home to our own hearts, and to ask ourselves what would our illustrious Mohammedan visitors discover if they, too, were to inquire of the signs and the measure of the presence and kingdom of Christ our Lord amongst ourselves. There can be no doubt that the Western civilisation which they have come to survey has on the whole been healthy and vigorous; but no less indisputable is it that if all who belong to it were true, genuine, and single-hearted adherents of its principles, it would be a million times more beautiful and glorious. Think what it would be if all our men had the earnestness of Wesley and the faith of Gordon, if all our women had the saintliness of Hilda and the self-devotion of Elizabeth Fry! Christ in His new kingdom of righteousness gave us many sources of health and regeneration, not alone for hereafter, but also for the present life. He gave us that sense of sin which is the essential antecedent to all improvement. He gave that inward peace and serenity and elevation which come from the sense of forgiveness through His atoning sacrifice. He gave us the secret of true happiness and real nobility of character, which is to be found in the complete and constant sacrifice of self. He gave us that pure domestic home-life which is the gift for which we never cease to thank Him best and most. He has given us the only true liberty, which lies in the conquest of self; the only true equality, which is in the oneness of all before God in the communion of the Christian Church;

the only true brotherhood, in the recognition of the sonship of all alike to God. He alone and none else has planted in us the enthusiasm of humanity and the law of love. He alone has taught us to devote ourselves not merely to what is good in each case, but to what is best. He alone has enabled us to be merciful and yet just, and to bind all society together by the blessed and beautiful power of forgiveness. By the communication of spiritual strength He has put it in our power daily to maintain and exercise all the graces which He has taught us. He has inspired and ennobled all our thoughts by the prospect of the unending future of happiness with Him beyond the grave. This is the glory of His Kingship; this is the light which shines for us over Bethlehem, and

Christians now the Light of the World.

of which He Himself set us the example.

But it is on us ourselves, under God, that the vitality of these principles and laws of life depends in their realisation. Are we conscious of them? Are we ourselves putting them into daily practice? Do we know the blessing of the conscience void of offence before God and before men? Have we experience of the daily renewing of the presence within us of the Holy Spirit of God? It is of little use for us to expect others to put the laws of the Kingdom of Christ into force before men if we are not ourselves actively engaged in the Christian warfare. It is of small avail for us to reckon up the privileges of Christian civilisation, if they are not to us ourselves individually the very breath of life. No star now shines over the human dwelling-place of Christ; no fresh illumination from heaven guides wanderers and inquirers to the shrine of God. On us is laid the dignity and burden of being the light of the world. God grant that every one of us may go forth to-day from our common worship in this place more determined than ever, by the help of His blessed Spirit, to extend His Kingdom and to maintain the splendour of its glory before men in that part of the battlefield where chiefly the struggle must be fought and chiefly the victory won, the secret paths and byways of our own hearts!

Indecision.

And another also said, Lord, I will follow Thee; but let me first go bid them farewell which are at home at my house. And Jesus said unto him, No man, having put his hand to the plough, and looking back, is fit for the kingdom of God.—ST. LUKE IX. 61, 62.

The Man who Wished to Say Good-bye.

HERE we have a third example in one passage of our Lord's way of dealing with half-hearted disciples. The man seems at first to be in earnest, yet he is not. He has not really made up his mind, and the friends at home would easily persuade him that he was a fool to think of taking such a step. He wished not to join Christ immediately on His voyage, but to go home and pick Him up some future day. It was an easy-going way of dealing with the Lord of life, which was terribly unsuitable. He little knew with what a tremendous crisis in his life he was trifling.

The Distress of the Half-Hearted.

Such a mistake it is which keeps back multitudes from that closer walk with God which would be to them such a wonderful happiness if they could only have it. They want to make the best of both worlds, and try to conciliate their friends and relations who are not devoted followers of Jesus. In every family circle there are worldly and careless members who have no great claim to the noble name of Christian. It is to retain the goodwill of these unsatisfactory people that many of us give up the inestimable comfort of a whole-hearted service of our Lord.

Folly of Divided Allegiance in the Aims of this Life.

Think how foolish this would be in any profession of civil life which any of us had chosen! Take, for example, a young man who has at one time taken enormous pains with his education, and has got, let us say, a first-rate start in the Army. At first he is diligent, and earnest, and all goes well. But by-and-by he gets into a groove of social amusements and pleasures, harmless enough in themselves, but which engross his time and turn him aside from the service of his country in the highest branches of his profession. The sacrifice of time and the continued struggles which he would have to make in order to fulfil his early promise and to do what is expected of him become irksome to him. He has begun to look back. His career is spoiled.

Compromise with the world is to Christians, of all other people, impossible. If Christians do not speak straight out for what is good and right and true, who is to do so? When questions of duty are brought forward, who is to support the cause of God if the Christian is to be silent? If questions of worldly approval and promotion and convenience are to weigh with the Christian, where

Impossibility of Compromise with the World.

48 INDECISION.

Decision and Resoluteness.

will the truth find any to proclaim it?

The man who would finally be accepted of God must be decided, firm, courageous, unflinching. He must not only set out well, but must endure unto the end. He must be very watchful over himself against hankering after the flesh-pots of Egypt which he has left once for all. Lot's wife is a standing monument to all ages, and warns us all not so much as to cast one look of regret at the emptiness and vanities which we have once renounced. A man who is guiding the plough through the rough, uneven clods of earth will make but a very poor line and a very slight impression if he look back at any call or cry or sight which he hears or sees behind him. A man who is working for the endless ages of eternity will never be judged fit for the kingdom of God if he be not continually intent on that which is before him and carefully following out his destined work.

Effects of Compliance.

Let those, therefore, who plead for worldly compromises and worldly gratifications and worldly considerations consider well their tendency and dread their effects. I grant that there are many things both seemly and innocent if thought of all by themselves. Yet a man in earnest for heaven will do well to avoid them, lest by means of them he should be ensnared and turned away from the straight and proper course. The man in a race will not only free himself from all incumbrances, but will gird tight about his loins the garment which would hinder the free motion of his limbs. So should we also cast away every weight, and the sin which either does or may easily beset us, and run with patience the race that is set before us. It would be better never to have known the commandment at all, than, having known it, to depart from it.

There will always be Unbelievers.

Do not be surprised at other people differing from you. As long as the world lasts there will be errors and mistakes. Never till the Kingdom of God comes will misguided men cease to trouble us. Do not think it worth while to temporise with them, or to make any compromise with them, or to look back from the truth which you have had the great privilege of believing. Do not think it worth while to make excuses and allowances for them, or to meet them half-way. Do not be afraid of exposing the hollowness and folly of their opinions. You are servants of truth. You cannot be loyal to the truth if you do not uphold it. If you try to make out that there is a great deal in what they have to say, you will only be destroying the truth and betraying your God.

Whether you are of a higher or a lower rank it matters not. You will surely find that if you will live godly in Christ Jesus, you will suffer persecution. David found this after he sat on the throne, no less than when he fled from the face of Saul. You must expect it. You must be ready for it even in its utmost possible extent, even to martyrdom itself. You must be prepared either to be bound or to die for the name of the Lord Jesus, if such a sacrifice should be called for at your hands. In nothing must you consult with flesh and blood. To follow the Lord fully must be the one deliberate and determined purpose of your soul. *Face the Consequences.*

Never are you to be weary in well-doing. If you draw back God can have no pleasure in you. You will draw back to certain and everlasting loss. You must be faithful unto death if ever you would obtain a crown of life. He *Result of Drawing Back.*

Tremendous Issues.

only who endureth unto the end ever will or ever can be saved.

And surely it is worth while to make certain of anything so tremendously important as our eternal state and welfare. Not much may be required of us, but trifling and hesitation are the two things which are out of the question. Doubtless the work will often prove heavy and fatiguing. Sin may be troublesome, but a persevering hold on God's truth can and will 'prevail. God has promised to each one grace sufficient for us. The more we labour, the greater our reward. Yes, the very work itself is one of the principal sources of peace and joy. It wonderfully helps to fit us both for this world and the next. We feel that there is a solid result beneath our feet, and we know that it is better for us to be living under God's laws and in His favour than in our own ways and under the lashes of a reproachful conscience. Who will make so distinguished a preacher of Christ, who will be so useful a servant of God by his example, as he who is altogether dead to the world? Who is so fit to join the saints above as he who already is one with them in their love to Him in Whom the whole creation lives and moves and has its being? Go on, then, forgetting what is behind, and reaching forth to that which is before, and soon shall the time come when you will not only rest from your labours, but when you shall actively and definitely, and with perpetual youth and freshness and vigour, enter into the joy of your Lord.

Confession and Denial.

Whosoever therefore shall confess Me before men, him will I confess also before My Father which is in heaven. But whosoever shall deny Me before men, him will I also deny before My Father which is in heaven.
ST. MATT. x. 32.

Christ's Claim to Unlimited Sovereignty.

WITH the calm confidence of a perfect royal majesty our Lord claims a final and universal sovereignty. There will be a great day when He who is now sending out His humble rustic disciples two by two will be enthroned in His eternal kingdom, and then before His Father and before the angels of God will acknowledge His faithful servants. And this discourse He extends beyond the Apostles themselves to all who should bear their witness to the very ends of the earth. And as with all other eternal laws, so here. The blessing on those who fulfil the laws has its corresponding use for those who do not fulfil them. Christianity is not a mere idea which we may choose or neglect as we like without any particular result. It is a choice which it is offered to us with the most tremendous consequences. To deny Christ on earth by word or deed, to live as if His work were nothing to us, is no mere loss to us of certain good and happy things which, after all, might be considered unnecessary to our welfare. It is far worse than this. It is infinite in the effect which it produces on us. Christ's word is once for all Light, the true Light, the only Light. To turn away from that Light shows that we are of the darkness, not of the light—that we love darkness rather than light, because our deeds are evil. It is an act on our part which itself pronounces judgment upon us. It leads as naturally as day leads to night, to Christ Himself denying us when He sits as our judge on the great white throne before His Father and the Holy angels and the countless assembled thousands of the whole human race.

Meaning of Denial.
And what is this denying Him? The number of those who have heard the name and message of Christ, and who have been baptized into His kingdom, may be divided into two. There are those who do not obey Him, and those who try to shape their lives according to His teaching. It may not always be easy to draw the line between the individual members of the two sets, but the spirit which animates the one set and the spirit which animates the other set are perfectly distinct and easy to be recognised by all candid and thoughtful persons.

The Test by Fruit.
Our Lord Himself has put us in a position to separate between the two, and without judging other people to know to which spirit we

ourselves belong. It would not be enough for us to say, "All who come to church and chapel, and join in public prayer and praise and profession of faith belong to one set, and all who do not go to church and chapel belong to the other set." Nothing could be more misleading. Christ has told us that there is such a thing as confessing Him with the lips while the heart is far from Him. He has given us a very different test. "By their fruits shall ye know them." "If ye love Me keep My commandments; by this shall all men know that ye are My disciples."

Our Lord does not mean to say that His disciples never show imperfections and faults, never are led into temptation, never stumble and fall, or have no room for progress. What He means is that on the whole they are earnest and serious in their loyalty to Him and in their belief in His work. They

Imperfections to be Expected.

differ from the others because their consciences are awake, they love light rather than darkness, they wish to do what is right, they think about His example and His principles, they try to get rid of their natural selfishness and to do all the good which comes in their way.

Daily Intercourse with the Worldly.

Our difficulty is that we are so much thrown about amongst those who do not care about our Lord. We meet them in every company, we read their opinions in every newspaper; wherever we go we find their selfish, worldly, bare, grovelling opinions in the front. It is very difficult always to realise that we have to do battle with these things, and to stand up for the principles and teachings of the Lord. These people of the world seem so like ordinary Christians, so like ourselves; they eat and dress the same, they look the same, they appear to do the same. We are not called upon to judge

CONFESSION AND DENIAL. 59

them; but if they constantly and habitually and without question or care do the things which Christ condemned and against which He warned us, then we know what spirit they are of, and we are bound decidedly to protest and to disengage ourselves from them. If their jokes and conversation and their way of looking at things imply a denial of Christ, then we can have nothing to do with them. If we come openly into contact with them, then we are bound not to submit, or be led by them, or be silent. We must stand up for the honour and truth and sovereignty of Him who died for us, that we should follow in His steps. Wherever pride is, or haughtiness, or extravagance or luxury, or selfishness, or self-indulgence, or impurity, or dishonesty, or hatred, or jealousy, or revenge, or party spirit, or suspicion, or malice, or base talking, or bowing down to opinions and teachings which are not the Lord's, there if we are present we must either withdraw or protest. We have to look out for the company of those who are kind, loving, true, unselfish, honest, scrupulous, strict in all their dealings, meek, gentle, forgiving, loyal to the Lord, and who would willingly do no wrong to man or woman. There we are safe. There we may be sure that all are gathered together in His name, whether He is mentioned or not. We shall be in no danger of denying Him.

Difficulties of Living in the World.
It is not always an easy thing. Though we are not to be of the world, God wishes us to remain in the world, and to leaven the world, and to show the world the example of our Saviour. He does not wish us to be peculiar, or to shun the busy haunts of our fellow men. But there always remains on us the high privilege, the unchangeable duty,

CONFESSION AND DENIAL. 61

even if it be the serious burden, of holding up the banner of the Lord. We must not acquiesce in the low base estimates and maxims of the world. We must not go to amusements where the Christian standard of right and wrong is not recognised. We must not willingly read books or approve of pictures which ignore the Redeemer of the world. We are not to be harsh and censorious, but we must be true. We are not to be severe, but we must be loyal.

Is not the reward enough? However sincere our contest may be, yet as the long struggle draws to a close, the best and bravest of us cannot but feel that we have greatly failed. As we lie down to die, if we are conscious of the crisis, the memories of old faults and sins will come crowding upon us. What a blessed surprise and delight to wake up in another world, and to

The Recompense of the Reward.

be welcomed and recognised by Him who is to be the Judge of quick and dead, our beloved Master and Saviour, not, it may be, as great heroes of virtue or pillars of the faith, because so high an honour is given to but few, but as humble and faithful servants who, amidst many temptations, and in much weakness, and conscious of many shortcomings, yet fought out the long fight, and in the strength of God, not in their own, strove for the honour of their Lord, and in the end overcame! What unutterable joy to be taken by the hand by Him, the Lord of all Bliss and Perfection, and brought amongst the innumerable company of rejoicing angels and the happy spirits of just men made perfect, into the unspeakable glory of the joy of the Lord!

A Good Conscience.

A good conscience.—1 Tim. i. 5.

Do not imagine for a moment that it is an idle discussion to ask what conscience is. If you understand this, you will be far more easily able to honour it, guard it, instruct it, and obey it. Now there is no difficulty whatever in showing what conscience means. The human soul is one and indivisible, and what are called its faculties are merely its way of treating different objects and occasions as they come before it. The soul is not like a chest of drawers, with one drawer marked memory, another drawer marked reason, another drawer marked sight, hearing, smell, taste or touch. The soul is one and the same living

What is Conscience?

agent, without parts or divisions, but acting differently with regard to different things. The soul is clothed with a body in order that it may make itself known during its lifetime in the world of sense, and in order that it may be tried and proved before it goes back into the world of spirits. It is because this body necessarily has different parts that people have been led into the mistake of thinking that the soul has different parts. It is really only the same living being acting through the different parts of the body as occasion requires. When the soul is occupied with the past, then we call its action memory, and it is putting the brain, without which at any time of course it can do nothing, into more immediate use. When the soul is loving, then we call it the heart, because love is exciting, and makes the heart beat quicker. When the soul is deliberating and comparing one thing with another, then we call its action reason. When the soul is looking at the external world, then we call its action sight, and it is using the eyes. When it is distinguishing different scents, we call its action smell, and it is employing the nostrils. So it uses the ears, the tongue, or the hand, and the employments it gives to these different servants or instruments are called the other senses. The soul can be injured and maimed through these servants. If the life is not healthy, and the brain becomes diseased. then the soul has no means of thinking on the past. The material record is destroyed, and as long as the soul is confined to the body it seems to depend on that material record of the brain. Or through drink or paralysis, or the unchecked indulgence of self-will, the reasoning power of the soul may be diminished. One by one its senses may be impaired. Still it remains, the living principle within, the lord and master of the cunning bodily frame, created by God in His own image, and beyond the skill of the wisest man to analyse or trace. Now then, just as the soul in looking back at the past is called memory, in looking at the present is called perception, in looking forward to the future is called hope, in loving is called the heart, in recognising things sweet is called smell, and the like; so when it looks at its duty, at things right and wrong, it is called conscience. It is very simple. Conscience is you yourself, in the inmost recesses of your mind; you, that living principle which is distinct from the whole universe; *you*, in the act of looking at things right and things wrong.

Mistaken Notions. People are given to talking about a little monitor, an inward judge, a guiding light, and they begin wondering where this monitor came from, and how it is that sometimes it is called good and sometimes bad, how it can sometimes be trusted and not at others. So they puzzle themselves. A poet asks:

Conscience, what art thou? thou tremen-
    dous power,
Who dost inhabit us without our leave,
And art within ourselves another self,
A master self that loves to domineer,
And treat the monarch frankly as the
    slave.

It is not good sense. If the poet had stopped to answer his own question in a reasonable way he would have said: "Conscience is I myself, my soul, the living principle that is called I, in the act of looking at things right and wrong."

Degrees in Conscience. When we think of it in this sober way as a matter of fact, we get rid of all those difficulties as to how conscience came or grew up. You would fancy by the way that some writers talk that conscience is a sort of little wayward spirit, sometimes coming dancing into the mind, then perhaps sitting for a short time on a sort of throne of judgment in the mind and trying to be very stern, then going to sleep for a long time, and then hopping and tripping off again. This, I say, is a mistaken notion. All that we know is, and it is quite enough for us to know, that we are each of us born with a capacity of finding out what is right and wrong just as we are born with a capacity to remember, a capacity to judge, a capacity to reason, a capacity to love, a capacity to taste, smell, touch, hear, and see. In an idiot this capacity would, of course, be very small indeed; but nobody who has been to an idiot asylum would deny that it is there. Again, in a child placed alone on a desert island, it would also be exceedingly small; it might almost dwindle away; still, as that child was not born without a soul, not without reason and reflection, if there was anything at all on that desert island to give it a choice between doing wrong and doing right, the power of choosing would be there. The soul, then, is born with this capacity, because its capacity is really and truly itself in regard to these questions of right and wrong. We allow, of course, that this character or capacity of the soul may be altered, lessened, or increased by many circumstances. All we care about knowing is that it is there. One thing that will alter it in different people is the character of the soul's parents and ancestors. That character impressed upon it in its birth as a legacy from past generations will not only make one soul more disposed than another towards different vices or different virtues, but that character from its parents and ancestors will make one soul inclined to think some things right or wrong which do not appear in exactly the same light to others. Another thing that makes a great difference in different souls in the act of considering right and wrong is their education. A Roman would have a very different idea of duty from a Hindu, or a Hindu from a Chinese, or all three from the idea of an Athenian; all the rest of the world would have great divergence in their thoughts about duty from the thoughts of duty that belong to the followers of Christ. And Christians have great differences among themselves according to race, religion, nationality, education. A Catholic peasant in Spain would have widely different ideas of what was right for him to do from the principles of a member of the Society of Friends in England. The soul, I say, will be greatly altered in its way of looking at these things by all these different circumstances and influences. This does not affect the real question. The capacity to judge between right and wrong may be greater or less according to the character of parents and ancestors; it may be greatly altered by race, religion, nationality, education. But in all cases it is there, inasmuch as the soul is there itself.

We have now got some distance on the way towards getting a reasonable answer to a practical question about conscience: How do I, how does my soul act, in thus considering questions of right and wrong? It is in this way. I look at different things of the same kind and class, and so exercise myself in comparison. I look at the past to see what has happened on such occasions in consequence of taking one line of action or the other; and so I exercise myself in memory, I look at the present to see what light I can obtain from my usual guides and principles as to duty, and thus I exercise myself in observation. I try to think what the results will be of acting in one way rather than another, and so I exercise myself in reason-

How Does Conscience Act?

ing. Lastly, I sum up the whole question, and thus employ my judgment. I then put the case before myself and warn myself of what is right and what is wrong. If I have given due weight to this process in past times, then I persuade myself very easily to do what is right, and I act upon my resolution at once. If I have not been careful in the past, if I have not been lucid in my deliberation and prompt in my decision, then I have all the greater difficulty; and perhaps the end is that I fail to listen to my own warnings, and allow myself to be carried away by the temptations of my own follies, impulses and passions. If I give way thus often at last I become very lazy in acting in my capacity of conscience at all; I stifle my conscience; I do wrong things without compunction.

Myself in My Capacity as Conscience.

Thus, then, it is that I act in my conscience—by comparing, by remembering, by observing, by thinking, by reasoning, and by judging. You may describe this shortly with Bishop Butler by saying that conscience is at one time a witness to what is right, at another time a regulator of our motives, at another time a magistrate sitting in judgment on our actions. But you are describing the same process in other language. It is myself in the various stages of my thinking about what is right and what is wrong. If the act be the act only of a little child, with small experience, and merely the dawn of an intelligence, it is in all points the same in kind as the action of the conscience of a sage.

We have now reached another point, and we see that when I act as conscience I warn myself, and set the whole case before myself; but when I decide and act the work of conscience is for the moment over, and I am employing myself in a new capacity—the *Myself in My Capacity of Will.*

function of will. While I was acting as conscience I was considering what was right and wrong; when I act as will I have done with considering, and I either obey my warnings or I set them at defiance.

Is a Less Enlightened Conscience Happier?

We have seen how much my attitude towards all questions of duty will differ according as I am born in one century or another, in this country or in that, or belong to one set of religious opinions rather than to some other set. Now a man might start up at this point and exclaim, "How much better to be born where the standard of conduct is not very high, and where, therefore, I should give myself very little trouble in my capacity of conscience!"

Real Happiness Consists in Conformity to the Will of God.

This is one of the most ignorant and faithless remarks that could possibly be made. Do you not know that not one single command has been given us by Almighty God except to increase our happiness? Do you not know that His commandments are not grievous, that each of them is not for His own will or pleasure or aggrandisement as such, but for our own welfare and happiness? Do you not know that it is only sin that brings a heavy burden, but that His yoke is easy and His burden light? Do you not know that His commandment is not the little, petty, niggling, irksome restrictions of men, but is exceeding broad? Do you not know that the more we put ourselves on the side of Him who is the source of all true enjoyment, and understand His will and act upon it, the more unalloyed will our happiness be? The really delightful life consists in the orderly and right employment of every faculty of body, soul and spirit; the nearer we are to God, the more we study His thoughts and wishes, so much the more surely shall we obtain this gift of self-command and this clear knowledge of our duty towards God, towards ourselves, and towards our fellow-men, this harmony between the loyal will and the enlightened conscience. Thus is the whole man at peace with himself, with the world, and with God. How else could this be obtained? How could any man be truly happy without it?

Will Conscience Grow Morbid by Being Obeyed? I can fancy I hear somebody objecting, Oh, but my conscience, my employment of myself, as you call it, in judging between right and wrong, would easily become too sensitive; it would soon grow to be morbid. You make a great mistake. Your conscience can only become too sensitive, can only become morbid, by trusting to men instead of trusting to God. If you trust to God alone as your guide and your enlightenment, you will find His wishes broad, simple, clear, wise, perfect, easy. You will be standing in the liberty wherewith Christ has made you free. If you look to men there are scores and hundreds all round you burning with eagerness to bring you into slavery; multitudes of good little books each with a set of rules for you to obey, and make your conscience sensitive and morbid; multitudes of good religious folk anxiously stretching out to you and saying, "Touch not, taste not, handle not." So it has been from the very beginning of Christianity, when the Jews tried to interfere with the liberty of the Gentiles. So it has been even with the best human arrangements ever since. So it is abundantly now, so it will be for ever. What says the Word of God? Stand fast in the liberty wherewith Christ hath made you free. Be not so foolish as to submit yourself to the ordinances of men, and then your conscience will grow neither sensitive nor morbid, but will be healthy, manly, strong, and wise.

Conscience Needs Training.

We have seen what conscience is, we have seen how it acts, we have seen whence it derives its inspiration, we have seen how far better it is to have an enlightened than a dark conscience, we have seen why it is that consciences ever grow over-sensitive and morbid. Observe in conclusion that you cannot hope all at once to get a conscience always void of offence toward God and toward men. What does St. Paul say? "Herein I exercise myself." I practise myself. Like every other virtue of the soul, obtaining a conscience enlightened, strong, and unstained is a matter of growth and habit and discipline. When I was describing the different faculties of mind employed by the soul in an act of conscience, no doubt you thought I was making out too long a process. All these different acts of mind are there, but it is habit, exercise, education, that, when they are all combined in an act of conscience, makes that act seem like a flash of inspiration. At first conscience is slow, weak, and ignorant, because I am slow, weak, and ignorant. Sometimes I have thrown myself back by wilful sin, and then I have not the same confidence, heart, or courage next time in warning myself. But when I repent Christ will wash my conscience clean through His blood. When I pray the Holy Spirit will come and give me power. When I study the Word of God, He will bring home its lessons to my soul, and they will be there to help me. By steady persistence in well-doing, in spite of many falls, by determined trust in my God in spite of many disappointments, I shall grow quick to know what is right, and strong to do it!

Glimpses of Peace.

Being justified by faith, we have peace with God through our Lord Jesus Christ.—ROM. v. 1.

Golden Hours.

"Do you not bear away with you," said Prudence to Christian in our immortal English allegory—"do you not bear away with you some of the things that in your former life you were conversant withal?" "Yes," was the reply of the pilgrim, "but greatly against my will, especially my inward and carnal cogitations with which all my countrymen as well as myself were delighted. But now all those things are my grief, and might I but choose my own things, I would choose never to think of those things more; but when I would be a-doing of that which is best, then that which is worst is with me." "Do you not find sometimes," said Prudence, "as if those things were vanquished which at other times are your perplexity?" "Yes," answered Christian, "but that is seldom; but they are to me golden hours in which such things happen to me." "Can you remember," continued Prudence, "by what means you find your annoyances at times as if they were vanquished?" "Yes," said Christian; "when I think what I saw at the Cross, that will do it. And when I look upon my broidered coat, the robe of the righteousness that is by the faith of Christ, that will do it; and when I look into the roll that I carry in my bosom, the Word of God, that will do it, and when my thoughts wax warm about whither I am going, that will do it." "And what makes you so desirous," asked Prudence, "to go to Mount Zion?" "Why there," exclaimed the pilgrim, "I hope to see Him alive that I did see hang dead on the Cross, and there I hope to be rid of all those things that to this day in me are an annoyance to me; there they say there is no death, and there I shall dwell with such company as I like best. For, to tell you the truth, I love Him because I was by Him eased of my burden; and I am wearied of my inward sickness, and I would fain be where I shall die no more, and with the company that shall continually cry, 'Holy, Holy, Holy.'"

Ebb and Flow.

In these homely words there is a powerful illustration of that magnificent chapter in St. Paul's Epistle to the Romans which is one of the most precious parts of our Christian inheritance. It must appeal to the experience of every one of us. For while, thank God, nothing can be more true than this, that when in all humility we have felt assured of the forgiveness of our sins through the blood of the Lamb of God, there steals into the soul a sense of rest and peace and tranquillity and unutterable joy before which every other sort of happiness fades away into a pale shadow, like the delight of a child when its tears are dried by a mother's love, and though its breast still heaves with the past passion of grief, its shining eyes show that it has forgotten it all in its new consolation, yet this other fact is, alas! equally true, that not in this life are all our habits, tastes, imaginations, desires, and occupations so entirely transformed as to leave us always in harmony with such moments of high blessedness. We cannot expect it. We still have to lead our life on earth with the same mental and bodily apparatus as before. The Holy Spirit will indeed be with us, but we shall feel His benign presence at one time rather than another. This is one of the trials, but it is also one of the necessities of the Christian life. Were it not so, we might become presumptuous and careless. We are not allowed to count ourselves to have apprehended. Suppose, for example, a mission has been, by God's blessing, arousing many souls in a parish. Some burning son of thunder has day after day been upholding the Cross. His words have been living with the very Spirit of God. Crowds have come to listen to him. Their emotions have been stirred; they have felt a Divine conviction of sin. They have wept and prayed. The eyes of their understanding have been opened, and they have seen the glory of the Son of God taking away the sin of the world. They have felt a change come over them, and they hope and believe that all things are become new. Such a time of conversion cannot be better described than in the words of the Book of Job, for it is no new thing, but as old as the oldest of God's dealings with men. "*If there be a messenger with thee, an interpreter, one among a thousand, to show unto man God's uprightness, then God is gracious unto him, and saith, Deliver him from going down to the pit: I have found a ransom. His flesh shall be fresher than a child's: he shall return to the days of his youth; he shall pray unto God and God will be favourable unto him: and he shall see God's face with joy; for God will render unto man His righteousness.*" And then that specially gifted messenger, that interpreter so rich in blessings, that one among a thousand, goes away to visit other places, to speak to other souls, and the penitent sinner who has through his words seen so much has to go out again into the world of everyday. He has to meet his old imperfect, commonplace companions, he has to be busy with his old humble, uninspiring occupations. His old temptations and thoughts come back, and he yearns once more for that moment of high rapture which he had when first he saw that God was gracious unto him and had found a ransom. This, I say, is the experience of each of us.

> Where is the blessedness I knew
>   When first I saw the Lord ?
> Where is the soul-refreshing view
>   Of Jesus and His Word ?
> What peaceful hours I once enjoyed !
>   How sweet their memory still !
> But they have left an aching void
>   The world can never fill.

Experience Worketh Hope.

Now what St. Paul reminds us of in this text is that just as God has a never-failing store of *grace and power* for the strengthening and reviving of our spiritual life, so also He has an inexhaustible reserve of *peace* from which we have only to draw in order to be reassured and comforted. He has a process not mechanical, but in the natural order of His providential dealing with the soul by which this peace, this highest consciousness of the spiritual life realising itself in unbroken union with God, is maintained. It is the living Lord, with Whom we may be in daily, in hourly communication, and who will by His presence and power purify, ennoble, in a word, Christianise all our surroundings in all their manifold relations to our souls. "*By Him,*" St. Paul says, "*by Him we have access by faith into this grace wherein we stand, and rejoice in hope of the glory of God. Hope begins, accompanies, continues and ends the scale of our progress until it is itself swallowed up in glory.*" Whatever we have already attained of spiritual stability and security and satisfaction, the secret of maintaining that achievement is ever and immediately to hope for more. And the very trials and disappointments themselves are all only so many mercies of God from heaven if they do but drive us back away from trusting in ourselves to look more earnestly and abidingly to that Cross from which our happiness first arose; if only like the raging storm of wind sending down the roots of the oak deeper into the earth at each wrench of the trunk and the branches, they make us more firmly fixed in the certainty of our faith. "*Not only so,*" says St. Paul, "*but we glory in tribulations also; knowing that tribulation worketh patience, and patience approvedness, and approvedness hope.*" Prosperity, it has been said, is the blessing of the Old Testament, adversity of the New. If everything were smooth and smiling at all times, God's most wise and most gracious discipline would be baulked. We have to learn patience in order that our will may in each of its relations be chastened to a thankful submission to His. And when we have learnt that lesson of patience there comes the sense of approvedness; the result of endurance is to test, confirm, and refine the higher and better elements of faith. We feel that our own state of mind has received a corresponding answer from God; that it has been recognised, that it has made a change in our condition, and that we are stablished, strengthened, settled. Then Hope in her robes of rainbow hue, linking earth and heaven together with her radiant smile, who has been accompanying us all through, leaps forth again in tenfold brightness, reminds us once more of all that has been done for us by our Saviour, recalls once more His gentle, tender, wise, friendly, most gracious and most real presence, and cleans the windows of our hearts so that we may again see the beauty of what lies before us. At first we hoped from what we were told; now we hope from what we know. Our early hope was that of the novice; this is nearer the hope of the veteran. This hope will never disappoint or deceive or make us ashamed. We shall never feel that we have been misled by an ill-grounded enthusiasm. Its object is quite certain. Not only will the issue prove it to be well-founded, but we have a supreme fact of spiritual consciousness to depend on in the present, *because the love of God is shed abroad in our hearts by the Holy Ghost which is given unto us.* That is all we need ask or expect. That is enough. However far we may sometimes seem to ourselves to be removed from the ecstacy of perfect peace, we have but to trust to God and to His plan and process for us. We have but to remember that Jesus liveth for evermore. We have but to accept all our experiences with thankfulness, asking God to make the best use of them. We have but to run with patience the race that is set before us. We have but to wait God's time. Then comes approvedness, then comes a purer and truer and brighter hope, and the deep conviction that the everlasting arms are about us because our spirit is buoyed and calmed and controlled and strengthened and sustained by the spirit which we know to be the living presence of God. When it is good for us God will give us such higher glimpses as will cheer and strengthen our souls in their onward course.

Charles Wesley's Evidence.

Sometimes a light surprises
   The Christian while he sings ;
It is the Lord who rises
   With healing on His wings ;
When comforts are declining,
   He grants the soul again
A season of clear shining
   To cheer it after rain.

In holy contemplation
   We secretly then pursue
The theme of God's salvation
   And find it ever new ;
Set free from present sorrow
   We cheerfully can say,
Even let the unknown morrow
   Bring with it what it may.

It can bring with it nothing
   But He will bear us through ;

> Who gives the lilies clothing
>   Will clothe His people too;
> Beneath the spreading heavens
>   No creature but is fed;
> And He who feeds the ravens
>   Will give His children bread.
>
> Though vine nor fig-tree neither
>   Their wonted fruit shall bear,
> Though all the field shall wither,
>   Nor flocks nor herds be there,
> Yet God, the same abiding,
>   His praise shall tune my voice,
> For while in Him confiding
>   I cannot but rejoice.

God's Opportunities not Haphazard.

But what I would further say is this. God has not left to mere haphazard these opportunities for repairing the breaches which the world makes in the spiritual fortifications of our souls. You remember how Prudence asked Christian if he could remember by what means he found his annoyances at times as if they were vanquished? "Yes," said Christian, "when I think what I saw at the Cross, that will do it; and when I look upon my broidered coat, that

will do it; and when I look into
the Roll that I carry in my bosom,
that will do it; and when my
thoughts wax warm about whither
I am going, that will do it." We
should, indeed, be fatally presumptuous if we did not remember that
God has left us appointed means of
grace, by diligent and humble
attendance on which we may hope
for continual revival, and for
renewed gleams of spiritual light.
He has left us the Christian
society, the living witness and
pillar of the truth. He has granted
us the ministry of reconciliation, in
raising up generations of humble
men to serve their brethren in
holy things. He has given us the
preaching of the Word so that
some of us may even in foolishness
and weakness, yet in loyalty and
faith, from time to time put the
rest in mind of things which they
might forget. He has put into our
hands His Holy Word, from which
we can never return without an

answer. Again and again that Word is attacked, and He gives us abundant confirmation of its truth. And He has offered us access in public and in private to that throne of grace where He delights to grant us His blessings far more abundantly than we deserve or venture to desire. And He has bequeathed us those simple ordinances of Christian initiation and Christian fellowship where at the quiet memorial of His Holy Supper we may gather into one all our highest aspirations and longings, where we may pour out into His ear all our hopes and our fears, where we may revive all our happiest recollections and associations, where in the silence of His house of prayer and none hindering us we may have uninterrupted intercourse with Him as friend with friend. There we are invited to think of what we saw at the Cross. That will do it. There we are told to look upon our broidered coat, the robe of imputed righteousness, the robe of sanctification, the robe of holiness that is worn by the obedience of faith. That will do it. There we are reminded of the most precious sentences and teaching of the Roll that is in our bosom. That will do it. There if anywhere our thoughts wax warm about whither we are going. That will do it. Ill for us will it be if we neglect these regular occasions for sitting at our Saviour's feet and worshipping Him with all the gratitude, with all the strength and purpose and adoring love of a heart that has known the burden of sin, of a heart that knows the bliss of peace, and that longs evermore to have the message repeated, and again repeated, which was given to Mary Magdalene: "Thy faith hath saved thee; go in peace." That was the consolation in his closing years of the great Christian moralist of the last century, Dr.

Johnson. He was a man of strong passions, of high principles, and a tender conscience; and when the remembrance of our Saviour's words came into his mind he repeated them in the Greek with great energy, saying, "The manner of this demission is exceedingly affecting." That is what we may hope for if the Holy Spirit be with us at the Lord's table.

Peace to those who Differ.

As one practical conclusion I would appeal to all Christian men and women to drop from their minds at that high moment of devotion and spiritual union the spirit of theological and ecclesiastical censure and recrimination. There will always be differences of theory and diversities of ritual; the how and the when, the more and the less. It is right that we should each have our own theory, intelligently analysed and grasped, our own method, properly based and authorised. But we need not at such a moment criticise the traditions and customs of others. It is the same Divine Being who is worshipped in the Christ who comes to us in His own covenanted ordinance. It is the same Lord who is over all, rich in mercy, waiting to bless, ready to pardon all our human misinterpretations and mistakes, so long as we have faith to be healed!

The True Meat.

My meat is to do the will of Him that sent Me, and to finish His work.
St. John iv. 34.

As the poor woman had forgotten her pitcher, so our Lord had forgotten His hunger. The deeply absorbing interest of that memorable conversation had lifted His whole human nature, weary as it had been before, into a state of rapt thought and heavenly contemplation. He had just proclaimed Himself for the first time to be the Messiah. He saw how the Samaritans would be flocking round Him at the woman's report; how they would be converted, how they would form the beginnings of a church. So when the disciples wanted Him to reward their expedition by taking food, He felt no

THE TRUE MEAT. 99

need of bodily support. He answered in one of His deep enigmatical sayings which were intended to be remembered for ever: "I have meat to eat that ye know not of." You, My disciples, unspiritual as yet, are busy about the things of this life; some day it will be different even with you; but it is a loss to you now that you cannot yet see the inner life of things. I, the Son of God, have the privilege and the burden of seeing these things as man cannot see them; and so great is the privilege that the burden is altogether absorbed in it. My weak human nature is sustained and buoyed up by the glory of the reality that you cannot see. I have meat to eat that ye know not of.

Again the disciples mistook, and talked to themselves about it, instead of asking Him. "Hath any man brought Him aught to eat?" passed from mouth to mouth. They were incredulous, almost captious. They were not yet accustomed to that Divine enigmatical manner which made it easier for the Holy Spirit afterwards to recall the sayings to their hearts.

The Wages of the Reaper.

But our Lord, with His usual gracious gentleness, did not leave them in doubt. "My meat," He explained, "is to do the will of Him that sent Me, and to finish His work. Three years I have got to do it in, and while you have been away at the little shops of the town I have been doing that work. Already what I have been doing is beginning to tell. Look at that poor woman hurrying away into Samaria. There is the firstfruits of My labour." And then He gave them an illustration, as usual in the form of a parable, to make them remember it. "Look at those green fields," He said; "you think the harvest is a very long way off—say at least four months. Very well. What would you say if I were to tell you that you were mistaken in thinking them green, that they were covered with full-grown grain which was not merely golden, for it has passed that stage; not merely brown, for it has passed that stage too; but actually in the very last stage of ripeness of all, positively white and ready at this very minute to be cut by the sickle? Yet that is actually the case in My meaning. I mean the hearts of the Samaritans, the heart of that poor woman. It is these that are ripe for the harvest, little as you think it. You think her a poor outcast, you think them ordinary townsfolk, just as you think the fields green. You do not see that she has in this short hour been converted from her evil ways, and that her companions are on the very point of being converted too. That is the harvest. That is the glorious work I have to do. That is the work that sustains and inspires and cheers Me against all bodily fatigue and faintness. And you, too, are now called to that work. Hitherto you have thought only about following Me. If you follow Me you must be as far as you can as I am. You, too, must have a harvest. You, too, must have a work. You, too, must find your work so absorbing as to make you almost forget your daily food. Your first harvest will begin just now. You will have the delight of keeping company with these new-born Samaritans. They will believe Me, and will want to hear all about Me. You will have the pleasure of telling them. For the next few days you will be in a state of great happiness. You will be helping these poor people to see the truth and love it. At many a hearth in yon little town you will be welcome and honoured guests, recounting all that has happened since you first began following Me. You will have your experience of the reward there is in reaping. He that reapeth receiveth wages, and gathereth fruit unto life eternal, that both he that reapeth and he that soweth may rejoice together. The wages of the reaper is the joy—the greatest that the heart can know—of gathering others, as men gather corn into the garner, into eternal life. You will be the reapers, and that will be your joy. I have been sowing while you were buying, and now you are going to share in the results. You offer Me your poor perishing food; I promise you the imperishable joy of winning souls. This view makes that old saying more than ever true, 'One soweth and another reapeth.' I shall be gone from the earth before you reap the full harvest of Samaria. Philip, the deacon, will be a chief reaper, and Peter and John will be there. It matters not to Me. The joy of sowing is enough. I know what I am doing, and I see its fruits. The joy of sowing and the joy of reaping is all one. Even now you will be reaping in yonder little town what you have not sown. The prophets prepared the way for Me, and I have begun finishing, fulfilling, and interpreting the work of the prophets. You have done nothing but listen to Me. I sent you to reap that whereon ye bestowed no labour; other men laboured, the prophets and I Myself; ye are entered into their labours. It is a glorious calling for you; enjoy it and fulfil it! Let the thought that you are carrying out the dreams of the prophets nerve you to courage, energy, and loyalty! It is a happy beginning, here in Samaria; let the enjoyment of it be to you a foretaste of that great honour which is to be yours through life, and which will make you hereafter shine as the stars for ever in the kingdom of My Father!"

So, in the light of subsequent events, we may interpret the brief heads of our Lord's discourse on the unseen meat and the spiritual harvest.

The Enthusiasm of Duty.

My brothers, the feeling that the ordinary occupations and the ordinary pleasures of life are of so little importance that even the taking of food, which seems to be the most necessary of them all, is as nothing at all in comparison of doing the will of God and of finishing His work—this is the spirit which has been the strength of the best lives and noblest deeds of humanity. This was the spirit which carried the glorious Apostle of the Gentiles through his boundless labours, strengthening him for all his ceaseless watchings and fastings, his dangers and journeys, and enabling him to spread far and wide among the nations the knowledge of the unsearchable riches of Christ. This was the spirit that made

Alfred the greatest of Englishmen—the pursuit of duty which devours all else, the devotion to God's work in the world which never rests or is contented with what it has done. This was the spirit of Luther, which made him buy the truth at all hazards and sell it not for peace or favour; which absorbed him night after night in the study of the Word; which emboldened him to speak before emperors and kings; which accomplished his splendid revolution in the religious thought of Europe. This was the spirit of Tyndale, which, in spite of obstacles which seemed insurmountable and without number, made him pour into this country those copies of the Word of God which have been ever since blessed in their results beyond calculation. This is the spirit which made the tears run down the cheeks of hardened, ignorant miners and peasants at the preaching of

Whitfield and Wesley, and founded in the dark places of England, in many a sinful village and many a gloomy mine, a religious life which has grown and flourished with the grace of God. This was the spirit of Henry Martyn and Samuel Marsden, and Noble and Fox, and the heroes of English missions, and which, after centuries of neglect, has lit the flame of the lamp of God in the very ends of the earth. This is the spirit that enabled Hampden and Cromwell to stem the growing tide of tyranny, and plant the liberties of England firmly in the soil for others to nurture and bring to perfection. Inspired by this spirit, Chatham and Pitt played their gigantic parts in European history, and freed the interests of the world from ambitious oppressors. It was this heroic enthusiasm for duty which produced Havelock and Outram and Clyde at the hour of direst need. This it was which burned in the breasts of Bacon and Newton and Faraday and Harvey and Simpson, and empowered them to throw wide open for human advancement and human improvement the awful gates of knowledge. This, even when not directed to the highest and divinest ends, has made every real student, every zealous patriot, every successful soldier and seaman, every genuine artist and musician. Applied to such ends, it has ennobled and beautified life; applied as our Master applied it to the will of God, it has regenerated the world.

Stern daughter of the voice of God!
  O Duty! if that name thou love,
Who art a Light to guide, a Rod
  To check the erring and reprove;
Thou who art Victory and Law
When empty terrors owerawe,
From vain temptations dost set free,
And calm'st the weary strife of frail
    humanity!

Stern lawgiver! yet dost thou wear
  The Godhead's most benignant grace;

Nor know we anything so fair
  As is the smile upon thy face:
Flowers laugh before thee on their beds
And fragrance in thy footing treads;
Thou dost preserve the stars from wrong,
  And the most ancient heavens through
     thee are fresh and strong.

To humbler functions, awful Power,
  I call thee: I myself commend
Unto thy guidance from this hour;
  O let my weakness have an end!
Give unto me, made lowly wise,
The spirit of self-sacrifice!
The confidence of reason give;
  And in the light of truth thy bondman
     let me live!

Blessing through Self-sacrifice.

Here, then, lies the question that we must ask ourselves this day, What is our meat and drink? Is it merely to get through the day without discomfort? Is it to while away the time with variety and pleasure? Is it to get out of life all the pulsations of delight possible to us? Is it to give ourselves up to the sinful lusts of the flesh? Is it mere worldly success? Is it the applause and esteem of our fellow-men? Is it admiration, or vanity, or fame? Is it for wealth and honour and prosperity? Is it to found a name and to leave a reputation? Is it merely work for its own sake, or success for its own sake? Is it even a desire to do well for your children?

If our meat, our object in life, our chief aim, be these or any of these, then we have not yet become followers of Christ, nor have we yet learnt the secret of happiness.

Something nobler, something higher, truer, purer, has to be grasped. To have the blessing of God on our lives, which is the only thing worth caring about, we have to sacrifice ourselves. We have to live for God, and for the good of others. That is revealed to us as the true ideal; it is proved to us by the noblest careers. What is our ruling thought, our absorbing passion? That is the test! Or let us ask ourselves whether we have any desire at all for doing God's work and doing good to others. Is such a feeling unknown to us? Do we prefer easy lives, our own way, comfort, luxury, the friendship of the world? What an ignoble existence! What a Christless soul! What a certainty of disappointment and misery!

> Yes, better 'tis to die
> Than from the strife to fly;
> Be thou a hero on the field,
> With arm close bound to duty's shield;
> Aloft the standard hold
> Among the true and bold;
> Turn not ignobly recreant back,
> A traitor on life's holy track;
> But fall on valiant ground
> And be with honour crowned;
> A rank among the faithful claim,
> And leave on earth a blessed name
> That kin and kind may hold
> Above the price of gold!

There is little satisfaction in being half-Christian, without giving ourselves up wholly to the spirit of Christianity. There is little vitality in that faith which leaves the heart in the possession of the world, which does not change the nature, which does not produce in us the mind of Christ. Half the evils of mankind are owing to a merely outward Christianity. What is the reason why the earth is not yet evangelised? The sloth and faintheartedness of Christians. Why is the name of Christ blasphemed every day by unbelievers? Because of the self-seeking, inconsistency, and incompleteness of the professed servants of our Master. Why are so few great things done among us for Christ? Because we are not fired, as we should be if we gave ourselves wholly up to the Spirit of God, by the holy enthusiasm of His servants. That is indeed an ambition which gilds all it touches, and ennobles all who embrace it. Said Schiller:

What shall I do to be for ever known?
    Thy duty ever.

This did full many who yet slept unknown?
    Oh, never, never!
Thinkest thou perchance that *they* remain unknown
    Whom *thou* knowest not?
By angel trumps in heaven their praise is blown.
    Divine their lot!

What shall I do to gain eternal life?
    Discharge aright
The simple dues with which each day is rife?
    Yea, with thy might!
Ere *perfect* scheme of action thou devise,
    Life will be fled,
While he whoever acts as conscience cries
    Shall live, though dead.

Without haste, without rest,

So said a greater German poet still, the wise Goethe:

Bind the motto to thy breast;
Bear it with thee as a spell:
Storm or sunshine, guard it well!
Heed not flowers that round thee bloom,
Bear it onward to the tomb!

Haste not! let no thoughtless deed
Mar for aye the spirit's speed!
Ponder well and know the right—
Onward then, and prove thy might!
Haste not! years can ne'er atone
For one reckless action done.

Rest not! Life is sweeping by,
Go and dare, before you die;
Something mighty and sublime
Leave behind to conquer time!
Glorious 'tis to live for aye
When these forms have passed away.

Haste not! rest not! calmly wait;
Meekly bear the storms of fate!
Duty be thy polar guide;
Do the right whate'er betide!
Haste not! rest not! conflicts past,
God shall crown thy work at last!

Do not mistake me. Few of you are called to be St. Pauls o Luthers or Wesleys or Henry Martyns or Alfreds or Hampdens or Pitts. True heroism, real devotion to duty, can be shown as much in small things as in great. It is not the size of the action or the scope of the spirit at which God looks, but at its quality, its genuineness, its thoroughness, its purity, its truth, its single aim, its loyalty. It can be the daily meat to do the will of God and to finish His work in the humblest as well as in the highest sphere.

The Next Generation.

> Therefore shall ye lay up these my words in your heart and in your soul; and bind them for a sign upon your hand, that they may be as frontlets between your eyes; and ye shall teach them your children, speaking of them when thou sittest in thine house, and when thou walkest by the way, when thou liest down, and when thou risest up.
> DEUT. XI. 18, 19.

Responsibility of Parents.

"WHAT will parents be able to say to God at the Day of Judgment for all their neglect of their children in the matter of instruction and example and restraint from evil?" So wrote the great Archbishop Tillotson in the seventeenth century, and we cannot help feeling that such a question brings with it in these days even an increased sense of shame and regret.

Contemporary Obstacles to Parents' Influence.

The times in which we live are unfortunately marked by a general

THE NEXT GENERATION. 117

impatience of every kind of authority and a widespread sense of independence from all restraint. Conceit of our own opinions, however ignorant, reliance on our own judgment, however rash and ill-formed, this is the usual condition of young people as soon as they have learnt anything at all, or have in any way begun to earn anything for themselves. And as in our working families parents are very much away from home, are tired and exhausted when they return, do not care to keep up a perpetual struggle with their children, and are not perhaps themselves very sure of their own principles, example, and conduct, they too easily fall in with this spirit of rebelliousness and self-will, give up their duties, and lose all sense of the responsibilities which are laid upon them by God.

And yet, as members of the Kingdom of Christ, we cannot, in our more serious and thoughtful *Parents.*

Unconscious Influence of Parents.

moments, help acknowledging that to bring immortal souls into the world, or to receive them as a gift from God, as His blessing on our wedded life, whichever way we like to put it, is a privilege of the very highest order, and of the very weightiest importance. They are yours, with your instincts implanted in them by nature, copies of your character and habits. But for you they would not have been here at all. You are answerable for them before God. With you they are associated day and night during those years when impressions for good or bad are most easily formed, and when they are most deep and durable. "The hand of our parent traces on our feeble hearts those first characters to which example and time give firmness, and which perhaps God alone can efface." "In most cases," wrote an old Jewish Rabbi, "bad parents beget bad children; if parents, for instance, have no scruple about false coins and false weights, their sons are apt to commit the same crimes." "The parents are the first patterns which a child copies after. If they are lazy and worthless, the children are poor and destitute; if careless, they are slovenly; if ignorant, they are so likewise; if windy and pompous, they are conceited and vain." How easy it is for those who are accustomed to deal with children in the large elementary schools to tell from what kind of home they have come, and of what habits and character are their father and mother.

The indifference of parents, and particularly of fathers, which we all know to be very frequent among us, is to a considerable extent increased by the tendency of modern legislation. Our lawgivers, in their anxiety that children should be well brought up, and should have a fair start in

Some Results of Modern Legislation to be Considered.

life, have rather helped to form an unconscious sort of impression that the duties of the father have been in a large degree undertaken by the State. Compulsory attendance at school, for example, may be very necessary amongst an overwhelming population and unparalleled masses of streets and poverty, but it does help to make the father think that the duty of education lies rather with the State than himself. The constant feeding of large multitudes of children at some of the poorer schools may be very right and benevolent when there is so much want of employment, such an overflow of population, and such general wastefulness on drink; but it certainly goes to lessen the feeling of responsibility of the father, and may, in the end, only increase his carelessness and profligacy. The charitable clothing of children on a large scale, or in any but the most careful and well-considered manner, and with the utmost knowledge of details and varieties of circumstances, may be very kind and sympathetic, but it certainly tends to make the idle father fancy that the condition and comfort of his children is more a matter for the general public than for himself. It is, no doubt, necessary to protect children by law from working too early in mines and factories, from living in immoral houses, or from engaging in immoral occupations, or from the cruelty of such of their elders as are savage and brutal; but one side result of this is that amongst the ignorant the direct sense of responsibility is weakened. We have taken many necessary and unavoidable steps towards Socialism, but these steps should make us all the more anxious to increase the acknowledgment of individual duties, and to strengthen the sacredness of individual ties and obligations.

Inevitable Duty of Home Education.

First, then, remember that though the school may do much to give your children information and to improve their characters, it is your own duty, in the truest sense of the word, to educate them, to bring them up, to form their tastes and habits, to give them their principles; and from that duty you can in no way be absolved. It is your business to teach them obedience, reverence, purity, decency, prudence, caution, truthfulness, honesty, courage. It is your business to make them fear God and know His will. It is your business to check their faults, to improve their tempers, to be on the watch against all signs of evil, to give them the priceless blessings of self-control and unselfishness. When you have laid up all God's words in your own heart and in your own soul, and have bound them, as it were, for a sign upon your hand, that they may be as frontlets between your eyes, then ye shall teach them your children, speaking of them when thou sittest in thine house, and when thou walkest by the way, and when thou liest down and when thou risest up. " Few parents realise how much their children may be taught at home by devoting a few minutes to their instruction every day. Let a parent make a companion of his child, converse with him familiarly, put to him questions, answer inquiries, communicate facts—the result of his own reading, observation, or experience—awaken his curiosity, explain difficulties, the meaning of things and the reason of things; and all this in an easy, playful manner, without seeming to impose a task, and he himself will be astonished at the progress which will be made. The experiment is so simple that none need hesitate about its performance."

Physiological Subjects.

And here I would say very shortly that it is the duty of all parents to make their own children acquainted, at the proper age, with the simple facts of physiology and the laws and dangers of the human body (the Divine process of reproduction). Mothers should warn their girls on these subjects, fathers their boys. It is simply astounding that in this, a matter where children run such tremendous risks, where their whole happiness in life may be wrecked by one imprudent act or ignorant habit, parents almost invariably launch their children forth without one word of warning, and leave them to the chance and vicious information of their companions at school. If, when a girl or boy was likely to come under the influences of those of their own age who delight in indecent conversation, the mother or the father had already fortified them by wise and careful advice and information and warning on physiological subjects, then it is incalculable what an amount of misery and misfortune might be saved. The subject, when presented by a morbid and ignorant companion, is sure to have a most unfortunate and prejudicial effect on mind and morals. Introduced, on the contrary, by mother or father, or the family doctor, as an ordinary and necessary subject of instruction, it would lose its mischievous secrecy and unwholesome mystery, and knowledge and light would, even from the point of view of the natural life, very often prevent the most terrible disaster.

In establishing a life-long influence over your children, the great thing to avoid is impatience. While you are perfectly firm, you must at the same time be thoroughly kind and sympathetic. You must remember that once you were yourselves light-hearted chil-

Avoid Impatience.

dren, in whose heart folly and fun were bound up, and to whom mirth and mischief were the natural accompaniments of life. You must not expect old heads on young shoulders. A correction given in the heat of temper will be of no earthly use. To the boy it will not be the law of the father, but the law of the angry man, who happens to be stronger. When once your sons understand that you act deliberately on principle, and without passion, then they will be inclined to respect and obedience.

Win Confidence. You must endeavour always to win the confidence of your sons. If you do not take a constant friendly interest in their thoughts and pursuits, you must not be surprised that they very soon look upon you as complete strangers, outside the circle of their ideas and sympathies. It is by constant kindness and the magic touch of love that while they never cease to respect you they will at the same time learn to consider you their best, their wisest, their most considerate, their most forbearing friend.

It is very important, both from this point of view, and from your anxiety about the prosperity of your children, and from your acknowledgment of your duty as a citizen to your country, that you should early settle with them what line of life they will pursue, and direct all your efforts towards preparing them for it when once the point is settled. How can you leave a matter of such life-long importance to chance? Keep them at school as long as you can. Let their education, while you are about it, be as thorough and complete as it can be made. " Those parents act most wisely who have foresight enough to provide not only for the youth, but for the age of their offspring ; who teach them usefulness, and not to expect

Guide to the Choice of a Profession.

too much from the world; to become betimes familiarised with stern and actual realities of life." "I suppose it never occurs to parents that to throw vilely-educated young people on the world is, independently of the injury to the young people themselves, a positive crime, and of very great magnitude; as great, for instance, as burning their neighbour's house, or poisoning the water in his well."

Guard against Precocious Imitation of Men.

Try to keep them boys as long as you possibly can; do not let them prematurely ape the manners and habits and tastes of young men. A boy should never be allowed to smoke or to have courtships before he is eighteen. Provide him with other interests. Let him join institutions of young men for continuing his education both in mind and body. Get his attention engaged in the wonders of trade and commerce, the glorious and beautiful sights of this mighty empire. Encourage him to go as often as he can into the country, and to engage as much as he can in field sports—cricket, football, rowing, running, swimming, bicycling. Keep him from billiards and betting. Tell him the reasons why one occupation is useful and wholesome, the other bad and unsafe. Convince his understanding, and guide him by your own example.

Remember, after all, that though precept is good, example is better. "Parents, to do them justice, are seldom sparing of lessons of virtue and religion; in admonitions which cost little and which profit less; whilst their example exhibits a continual contradiction of what they teach." "Unless parents set a good example to their children, they will furnish a plain reason to be used by them against themselves; and this is to be feared, that if they have not lived an honourable life

Example more Powerful than Precept.

their sons will despise them and abandon them in their old age." "There is scarcely any one who cannot trace back his present religious character to some impression in early life, from one or other of his parents; a tone, a look, a word, a habit, or even, it may be, a bitter, miserable exclamation of remorse." How terrible if the ungodly character of your son, or the careless, unsatisfactory tone of your daughter, or their habit of neglecting the worship of God, could be distinctly traced to your own evil influence. "Parents of an unnoticed family, who, in their seclusion, awaken the mind of one child to the idea of love and goodness, who awaken in him a strength of will to resist temptation, and who send him out prepared to profit by the conflicts of life, surpass in influence a Napoleon breaking the world to his sway!"

www.ingramcontent.com/pod-product-compliance
Lightning Source LLC
Chambersburg PA
CBHW030400170426
43202CB00010B/1440